Edible Flowers

Edible Flowers

A KITCHEN COMPANION

With Recipes

KITTY MORSE

PHOTOGRAPHY BY OWEN MORSE

Ten Speed Press

To the memory of my grandmothers
Suzanne and Violet,
flower lovers both

Other works by Kitty Morse
Come with Me to the Kasbah: A Cook's Tour of Morocco
The California Farm Cookbook
365 Ways to Cook Vegetarian
Edible Flower Poster

1🕮

Ten Speed Press
P.O. Box 7123
Berkeley, California 94707
www.tenspeed.com

Distributed in Australia by Simon & Schuster Australia; in Canada by Ten Speed Press Canada; in New Zealand by Tandem Press; in South Africa by Real Books; in the United Kingdom and Europe by Airlift Books; and in Malaysia and Singapore by Berkeley Books.

Cover and text design by Beverly Wilson
Photo of Sunflower Pasta Salad on cover by Jonathan Chester/Extreme Images
Page composition by Jeff Brandenburg, ImageComp

Library of Congress Cataloging-in-Publication Data

Morse, Kitty.
        Edible flowers : a kitchen companion with recipes / Kitty Morse ;
    photography by Owen Morse.
            p.   cm.
        Includes bibliographical references (p.   ) and index.
        ISBN 0-89815-754-4
        1. Cookery (Flowers)   2. Flowers.
    TX814.5.F5M67   1995
    641.6—dc20   95-6708
                                                                    CIP

Printed in China
3 4 5 — 03 02 01 00 99

I know a bank whereon the wild thyme blows,

Where oxlips and the nodding violet grows

Quite over-canopied with luscious woodbine,

With sweet musk-roses, and with eglantine.

William Shakespeare,
A Midsummer Night's Dream,
act 2, scene 1

Contents

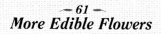

Acknowledgments

big thank you to all the herb and flower growers in San Diego County who taught me so much and gave so generously of their time: Stephenie Caughlin, Lo Cosenza, Jeanne Dunn, Andrea Peterson, Suilin Robinson, Luna Rose (who shared with me her love for Shakespeare's *A Midsummer Night's Dream*), Jan Sayles, Greg Smith, and Gerald Stewart; the staff of Nature's Nursery, Weidners' Begonia Gardens, and Exotica Rare Fruit Nursery; and Donna Greenbush of the Greenhouse, for providing me with out-of-season blossoms when I needed them. Thank you to my agent, Julie Castiglia, for believing in the project.

I want to thank botanical consultant Gilbert Voss for his invaluable assistance; edible plant specialist and writer Stephen Facciola, always a precious source of information; my friends Jan Chung and Anita Norman, who provided me with much-needed blossoms; and Lorena Jones, my editor at Ten Speed Press, for her patience.

And to my husband, Owen, my favorite photographer, ever patient and supportive, my everlasting gratitude.

Introduction

he use of flowers to flavor and garnish both sweet and savory dishes goes back to ancient times. Their use is enjoying a resurgence thanks in great part to upscale restaurant chefs who now commonly use an edible petal or two as the final touch to an elegant dish. Modern pastry chefs, like those of old, often rely on crystallized petals or candied flowers to add a touch of sweet nostalgia to their desserts.

Edible flowers, like vegetables, each possess their own characteristics. Among the better known we find the common dandelion, one of the bitter herbs mentioned in the Old Testament; the calendula, whose petals add a dramatic touch to frittatas or soufflés; and the nasturtium, favored in Mediterranean cuisine for its peppery tang. Nasturtium buds are also edible, and when pickled are sometimes used as substitutes for the more expensive capers. One of my favorite edible flowers, the delicate blossom of the exotic *feijoa* (pineapple guava), tastes just like the fruit of its ripe namesake. Certain varieties of geraniums add fragrance to cakes, frostings, or sorbets. Society garlic, as its name implies, is redolent of the "stinking rose's" pungent scent and permeates a dish with the heady aroma of garlic. Legend has it that Cupid, the god of love, once shot an arrow through a viola, and thus endowed the ubiquitous miniature pansy with aphro-disiacal properties.

Flowers have long been the secret ingredient in the manufacture of exotic potions and liqueurs. Herbalists the world over are well versed in the centuries-old art of preparing infusions from flower blossoms. Carnation petals, for instance, are one of the secret ingredients in

Chartreuse, a liqueur developed in France in the seventeenth century. England's Queen Elizabeth I is purported to have been quite fond of lavender tea, a mild sedative. According to the Roman writer and naturalist Pliny the Elder, the star-shaped, baby blue flower of the lush borage plant drove away melancholy and increased a man's courage. Chefs nowadays favor borage blossoms as much for their appearance as for their refreshing, cucumber taste. Pots of fragrant jasmine tea frequently accompany Asian dishes, while a small glass of fresh mint tea topped with an orange blossom is the traditional drink of North Africa. In Mexico, *jamaica,* a cool infusion made from the dried calyx of hibiscus flowers, is the drink of choice on a hot summer's day.

In this book, I offer a collection of easy-to-make recipes using commonly available edible flowers. I have attempted to render them as pleasing to the palate as they are to the eye. One important caution: make sure the flowers you choose have been grown naturally, without the use of pesticides. For that reason, flowers purchased from a florist and most nurseries are not acceptable. For best results, pick fresh edible blossoms with care at the peak of their bloom, preferably early in the day. When a recipe calls for using flowers "sparingly," one or two blossoms will suffice. When in doubt about the edibility of a particular flower, consult an encyclopedia of edible plants (see the Bibliography) or a horticultural specialist.

Arugula

*A*rugula (Eruca vesicaria *subspecies* sativa), *roquette or rocket by its other names, is one of the easiest greens to grow, with a tendency to take over a plant bed like a pesky weed. This lovely salad green, a member of the mustard family, has long been harvested in the wild in Mediterranean countries, but it is still relatively unknown outside gourmet circles in the United States. The tender, peppery tasting leaves of arugula are delicious on their own or mixed in* mesclun, *the blend of specialty lettuces and herbs often found in produce departments or farmers' markets. A warm spell will often trigger arugula plants to explode into a profusion of tiny pastel blossoms. Cut off the flowers and save the stems, and you may well get a second harvest a few months down the line. This soup makes use of a bountiful harvest of arugula.*

Arugula Arugula Soup

Serves 4

2 tablespoons olive oil
4 scallions, chopped
8 ounces fresh arugula leaves, rinsed and drained
3 cups chicken broth
1 cup cream
$\frac{1}{8}$ teaspoon ground mace
Salt and pepper to taste
1 cup arugula blossoms

In a large saucepan, heat the olive oil and cook the scallions until translucent. Add the arugula leaves and 1 cup of the broth, and cook, covered, until the leaves wilt, 2 to 3 minutes. Remove from heat and let cool. In a blender, purée the arugula leaves and their liquid until smooth, in increments if necessary. Transfer the purée back to the saucepan, and add remaining broth. Simmer soup 2 to 3 minutes (Do not bring to a boil), and stir in cream and season with mace, salt, and pepper. Heat through. Serve immediately, sprinkling each bowl liberally with arugula blossoms. Serve immediately.

Basil

mong the 150 varieties of basil (Ocimum basilicum) *identified so far, you will find those with names like cinnamon, lemon, or licorice, each one with a slightly different aroma.* Basil, which the ancient Greeks considered the king of herbs, today still ranks among the most-popular culinary herbs. From the minty green varieties to those with dramatically ruffled purple leaves, basil (which is a member of the mint family) stars in dishes the world over. In India, some basil varieties are even considered sacred and are dedicated to the gods Vishnu and Krishna. In Italy, the art of making pesto is held as highly as that of cooking perfect pasta. The French call basil herbe royale, or "royal herb," and use sweet basil to enhance the flavor of soups, stews, and salads. The following salad is especially striking when made with alternating slices of red and yellow vine-ripened tomatoes.

Red and Yellow Tomatoes with Basil Blossoms

Serves 4

2 large red tomatoes, sliced
2 large yellow tomatoes, sliced
½ pound mozzarella cheese, thinly sliced
3 tablespoons extra-virgin olive oil
1 tablespoon balsamic vinegar
2 shallots, very finely minced
Salt and pepper to taste
8 basil leaves, finely shredded
1 tablespoon basil blossoms

On a pretty serving platter, alternate red and yellow tomato slices with mozzarella slices. In a small bowl, mix the olive oil, balsamic vinegar, shallots, salt, and pepper. Pour the dressing over the tomatoes. Sprinkle with shredded basil leaves and blossoms. Serve at room temperature.

Begonia

I must thank my friend Gil Voss, a botanical and horticultural consultant, for inspiring this recipe. During one of our lengthy conversations concerning this book, Gil once mentioned that begonia stems could be substituted for rhubarb in a rhubarb pie! The idea stayed with me until one day I reluctantly cut down several gorgeous tuberous begonias (Begonia tuberosa) to try out the recipe. I waited until the blooms had started to fade, enjoying their brilliant colors until the very last, before turning the stems into a pie. Make sure you keep a flower or two for garnish, however.

Begonia Strawberry Pie

Serves 4 to 6

FOR TWO CRUSTS
½ cup butter, at room temperature
3 ounces cream cheese, at room temperature
1½ cups flour
A pinch of salt

FOR THE FILLING
3 cups begonia stems, stripped of leaves and flowers
1 cup sliced strawberries
4 tablespoons cornstarch
1¼ cups sugar
A pinch of salt
2 tablespoons butter

Petals from 1 or 2 begonia blossoms, for garnish
Several strawberries, cut in half, for garnish
1 pint heavy whipping cream, whipped

Preheat oven to 425°F. To make the crusts, in a bowl mix together the butter and cream cheese with a fork until well blended. Gradually add the flour and salt, mixing until you obtain a firm dough. With your hands, shape the dough into a ball, and cover with plastic wrap. Refrigerate 30 minutes. When the dough is firm, separate it into two equal parts. On a floured surface, roll out each ball into a circle to fit a 9-inch pie pan. Freeze one crust for later use.

In the meantime, cut begonia stems into ½-inch pieces. In a medium bowl, combine the begonia stems with the sliced strawberries, and set aside. In another bowl, mix the cornstarch with the sugar and the salt. Add this to the begonia/strawberry mixture. Pour the filling into a pie shell. Dot surface with butter. Bake at 425°F for 10 minutes, then reduce heat to 350°F and bake 25 to 30 minutes, or until crust is golden brown. Cool 15 minutes before serving. Garnish with begonia petals and strawberry halves. Serve with whipped cream on the side.

Borage

hese star-shaped flowers of borage (Borago officinalis) *have a cool, cucumber-like flavor, which can really enliven a salad or a sauce. In ancient times, it is said that Celtic* warriors drank a glass or two of borage wine before battle to increase their courage. Indeed, modern researchers have found that borage stimulates the production of adrenaline. Nowadays, some herbalists prescribe infusions of borage flowers as a diuretic, or to relieve fever and bronchitis, among other ailments. The leafy borage grows into full, graceful bushes that occasionally bear sky blue blossoms alongside bright pink ones, all on the same stem. The cool flavors of raita, *a sauce prevalent in Indian cooking, makes this a delightful accompaniment for poached seafood.*

Poached Salmon
with Yogurt-Borage Raita

Serves 4

FOR THE *RAITA*
1 eight-ounce container plain yogurt
2 tablespoons mayonnaise
1 medium cucumber peeled, seeded, and very finely diced
10 fresh mint leaves, finely chopped
1 teaspoon curry powder
Salt to taste
1 tablespoon lemon juice
½ cup borage flowers

FOR THE SALMON
1 cup white wine
1 bay leaf
2 scallions, whole
1 cup water
½ bunch parsley, tied with string
4 eight-ounce salmon steaks, trimmed and tied in cheesecloth

To make the *raita,* in a medium bowl mix yogurt, mayonnaise, cucumber, mint, curry powder, salt, and lemon juice. Stir in flowers just before serving. Reserve a few flowers for garnish. *Raita* can be made up to 8 hours ahead. It will keep 2 to 3 days in an airtight container in the refrigerator.

To poach the salmon, in a large saucepan, combine the wine, bay leaf, scallions, water, and parsley. Bring to a simmer (do not boil). Gently lower salmon steaks wrapped in cheesecloth into simmering liquid. Simmer 10 to 12 minutes, or until fish turns pink and flaky. With a spatula, transfer the salmon steaks to a serving platter. Drain liquid through a fine-meshed sieve and reserve for another use (in chowder, for instance). This dish can be served hot, at room temperature, or chilled. Before serving, top each steak with *raita* and fresh borage flowers.

Calendula

alendula (Calendula officinalis), *also called pot marigold, has had both culinary and medicinal applications for centuries. Throughout the ages, tinctures made from calendula blossoms have been used to treat headaches, toothaches, and even tuberculosis. The ancient Romans used calendula to treat scorpion bites, and soldiers in the American Civil War found it helped stop wounds from bleeding. In the sixteenth century, those who drank a potion made from marigolds were reputed to be able to see fairies.*

In mild climates, the bright flowers of the marigold paint borders and plant beds in infinite shades of oranges and yellows practically year-round. The dainty petals of the calendula, each one a floret in its own right, are commonly used to add a golden hue to soups, grains, or scrambled eggs. These savory roll-ups will keep well in the refrigerator, wrapped in plastic wrap, for up to three days. Large flour tortillas are some-times marketed as "burrito-size" tortillas in super-markets.

Turkey Calendula Roll-ups

Makes four 12-inch roll-ups

8 ounces cream cheese, at room temperature
2 tablespoons low-fat mayonnaise
1 tablespoon horseradish
2 to 3 teaspoons lemon juice
2 tablespoons diced sweet pickle relish
1 tart apple, peeled, cored, and finely diced
1 cup calendula petals
4 twelve-inch tortillas
8 ounces wafer-thin turkey slices or ham, if desired
Lettuce leaves, for garnish
Calendula petals, for garnish

In a bowl, blend the cream cheese with the mayonnaise, horseradish, lemon juice, and pickle relish. Gently stir in apple and calendula petals. With a spatula spread the mixture evenly over each tortilla. Cover spread with a single layer of turkey (or ham) slices. Roll up the filled tortilla, jelly-roll style. Cut immediately, or wrap tightly in plastic wrap and chill until serving. To serve, cut to desired thickness, and arrange on a serving platter over a bed of lettuce leaves. Sprinkle with additional calendula petals.

Chives

e have the Chinese to thank for introducing chives (Allium schoenoprasum) *to the Western world. This relative of the onion has been used in cooking for more than five thousand years. Early American colonists assigned magical powers to chives, hanging them in bunches at their front doors to ward off evil spirits. Chives are among the most common of herbs, and when you grow your own, you have the advantage of being able to use the aromatic blossoms as well as the slender stems in your dishes. "Chopping" fresh chives is easy to do with a pair of kitchen scissors.*

Herb Cheese Tart with Chive Blossoms

Serves 4 to 6

1 nine-inch pie crust (see page 7)
8 ounces cream cheese, whipped with chives and onions
3 ounces plain cream cheese, at room temperature
¼ cup sour cream
2 eggs, lightly beaten
12 large chive blossoms, separated into petals
Additional blossoms, for garnish

Preheat oven to 400°F. Roll out the dough carefully, and set it inside a greased 9-inch pie pan or a quiche pan. Refrigerate until ready to use.

In a large bowl, preferably with an electric beater, mix the herb cheese, cream cheese, sour cream, and eggs until smooth. Stir in chive blossoms. Pour into the prepared pie shell. Bake the tart in the preheated oven for 25 to 30 minutes, or until filling is puffy and light brown. Let stand 15 minutes before cutting. Decorate with additional fresh chive blossoms. Serve hot or warm.

Citrus

itrus (Citrus species and cultivars) petals tend to be quite waxy and have a pronounced flavor. Because of this, I recommend using them sparingly as a garnish. The ancestor of all citrus is believed to have originated in the Near East over eight thousand years ago. The ancient Egyptians used citrus as an embalming fluid; the Romans found certain varieties kept moths at bay. Citrus reached the shores of the New World thanks to sixteenth-century Spanish sailors who signed on with Ponce de León, the discoverer of Florida. He required all his crew members to bring along one hundred citrus seeds for planting upon landing.

All forms of citrus—from sweet tangerines the size and color of plump apricots, to the exotic, crimson-fleshed blood oranges—have long been cultivated in the Mediterranean Basin, and especially in North Africa. In Tunisia, a fresh citrus blossom often floats atop glasses of syrupy-sweet mint tea. This traditional Moroccan dessert, called mulhalbia, *makes use of a delightfully scented water distilled from orange blossoms. You can purchase it in specialty markets and in fine liquor stores.*

Mulhalbia *is reserved for festive occasions in Morocco.*

Moroccan Custard (Mulhalbia)

Serves 6

⅓ cup rice flour or cornstarch
2½ cups half-and-half
½ cup granulated sugar
1 cinnamon stick
2 tablespoons orange blossom water
¼ cup slivered almonds
2 tablespoons powdered sugar
1 teaspoon ground cinnamon
Whole citrus blossoms or petals, for garnish

In a medium bowl, whisk together the cornstarch with ½ cup of the half-and-half. In a large saucepan, bring the remaining half-and-half, the sugar, and the cinnamon stick to a low boil. Add the cornstarch mixture to the simmering cream on the stove. Stir in the orange blossom water, and cook, stirring constantly until mixture thickens enough to coat the back of a wooden spoon. Discard the cinnamon stick. Set thickened custard aside.

In a medium nonstick frying pan, toast the almonds, shaking the pan back and forth, until nuts turn golden. When cool, grind the almonds coarsely in a blender or food processor. In a small bowl, mix the ground almonds with the powdered sugar and cinnamon. Pour custard into a shallow platter and let cool slightly, 15 to 20 minutes. (Or it can be made up to 2 hours in advance and set aside on the kitchen counter.) Sprinkle with almond mixture, and dot with whole citrus blossoms. Serve at room temperature.

Daylily

s their name implies, daylilies (Hemerocallis *species and cultivars) live a mere twenty-four hours. This lovely and graceful native of Asia has long been prized for its color and* beauty, as well as for its culinary properties. The petals of the canary yellow, bright orange, and deep burgundy flowers are crunchy and fresh tasting, much like a crisp lettuce leaf. In China, the tiger lily buds (Hemerocallis fulva) *are dried, and added to soups or stir-fries. This bicolored chilled melon-mango mixture is a light and refreshing summer dessert. Substitute any variety of melon, if you prefer.*

Lilyed Melon and Mango Soup

Serves 4

1 mango, peeled and diced
1 medium cantaloupe, seeds and rind removed, cut into 1-inch cubes
¼ cup orange juice
1 cup sliced strawberries
1 tablespoon sugar
2 tablespoons Grand Marnier or Triple Sec liqueur
5 daylilies, rinsed and gently shaken dry

In a blender or food processor, purée the mango, melon, and orange juice in increments until smooth. Transfer to a bowl and set aside. Rinse out the blender and purée the strawberries, sugar, and Grand Marnier. Chill both purées separately for 2 hours before serving. To serve, ladle melon mixture on one side of a shallow soup plate. Ladle puréed strawberries next to it without mixing. Cut one daylily into thin strips. Sprinkle strips into each bowl. Decorate each bowl with a whole flower. Serve immediately.

Dianthus

ianthus (Dianthus *species and cultivars), come in myriad colors. This diminutive yet hardy member of the carnation family, adds a light nutmeglike scent as well as a colorful touch to salads, aspics, or herb butters. One legend holds that a carnation grew where each of Mary's tears landed as she walked along the road to Calvary.*

You can make the following herb butter with all sorts of flowers, including violas, calendulas, roses, violets, or society garlic. Make several rolls, and preserve them in plastic wrap in the refrigerator.

Dianthus Butter

½ cup dianthus blossoms, separated into petals
½ cup unsalted butter, at room temperature
Petals, for garnish

In a small bowl, mix petals and butter with
a fork. Cover a flat surface with plastic
wrap. Roll butter into a small log
shape with the help of the plastic
wrap. Pat the ends and sides of the
roll until they are smooth. Press
fresh flower petals around
the outside of log.
Wrap tightly in
plastic wrap and chill until ready to use.

Dill

he name *dill* (Anethum graveolens), *according to* Rodale's Illustrated Encyclopedia of Herbs, *is derived from the Norse word* dilla, *which means "to lull," alluding to the plant's soporific qualities. The ancient Greeks used dill as a cure for hiccups! Eastern and northern Europeans use this versatile herb's feathery fronds in a number of specialties, from marinated herring to goulash. Like shooting stars on a stem, the fragrant dill's tiny yellow blooms are a lovely garnish. They are also an excellent seasoning for soups or dips. Dill seeds are reserved for pickling or baking. The following appetizer is an adaptation of the traditional Swedish* gravlax.

Smoked Salmon Canapés
with Mustard and Dill Sauce

Makes 2 dozen canapés

2 tablespoons Dijon-style mustard
5 teaspoons sugar
2 tablespoons rice vinegar
1 tablespoon water
½ cup grapeseed or walnut oil
2 tablespoons fresh, chopped dill
8 ounces pumpernickel or whole wheat bread
4 ounces smoked salmon
¼ cup dill flowers

In a medium bowl, whisk together the mustard, sugar, vinegar, water, and oil until smooth. Stir in the dill. Set aside. Cut the bread into desired sizes and shapes. Cut salmon to fit sandwiches. Spoon a little sauce over the salmon. Top with a tiny sprig of dill and a few blossoms.

Geraniums

 eraniums (Pelargonium *cultivars)* were introduced to Europe from their native South Africa in the seventeenth century. Varieties such as the dwarf Martha Washington or Regal come in a wide range of shapes, from orchidlike to pansy-faced. Scented geranium leaves have the fragrance of pineapple, lemon, or rose, among many others. In Tunisia, an aromatic distilled water made from scented geraniums is a popular ingredient in pastries or drinks. For this recipe, I relied on the dwarf Martha Washingtons grown by Gerald D. Stewart of New Leaf Nurseries in Vista, California. Gerald owns one of the most extensive collections of scented geraniums in the world.

The recipe for the following cake is based on one for bûche de Noël, *or* yule log, handed down by my French grandmother.

Geranium Cake

Serves 10 to 12

1 cup water
2 cups scented geranium leaves (fresh or dried)
8 eggs
1 cup sugar
1 cup flour
2 teaspoons baking powder
Butter or shortening
12 ounces cream cheese, at room temperature
½ cup butter, at room temperature
1 sixteen-ounce box powdered sugar
Grated zest of 1 lemon
Petals from 2 to 3 dozen dwarf Martha Washington geranium flowers
Whole flowers, for garnish
Mint leaves, for garnish

First, either the day before or a few hours ahead of time, make some geranium tea. In a small saucepan, bring the water to a boil and add the geranium leaves (dried leaves yield a stronger aroma). Cover tightly, remove from heat, and let steep for 1 to 2 hours. Drain well through cheesecloth or very fine meshed sieve. Set tea aside, or keep refrigerated overnight.

To make the log, preheat oven to 400°F. In a large mixing bowl, preferably using an electric mixer at high speed, mix the eggs, 1 tablespoon prepared geranium tea, sugar, flour, and baking powder for 5 minutes. Using butter or shortening, generously grease an 11-by-15-inch baking sheet (nonstick preferred). Pour the batter evenly on the sheet, and bake on middle rack until top is golden brown, 8 to 10 minutes. Remove from oven. Cake will deflate as it cools. Wait until the thin skin covering the cake deflates, and then carefully flip baked cake onto a clean kitchen towel. Set aside to cool.

To make the icing, in a large bowl combine the cream cheese, butter, sugar, and 1 tablespoon geranium tea. Mix, preferably with an electric beater, until smooth. Stir in lemon zest. To assemble the log, with a spatula spread a thin layer of cream cheese mixture on the flat cake. Sprinkle with geranium petals. Using both hands, with the long side facing you, gently roll up the cake like a jelly-roll. Transfer to a serving platter. With a knife or spatula, frost the outside of the log with the remaining icing. Decorate with additional petals, whole flowers, and mint leaves. Chill for 2 hours before serving for easier slicing.

Hibiscus

he dramatic bloom of the hibiscus (Hibiscus rosa-sinensis cultivars) *is the state flower of Hawaii and is also common to Mediterranean climates. Hibiscus is a native of Africa and parts of Asia, where bushes often grow to twenty feet tall. In Mexico, the fleshy, dried calyx of* jamaica (Hibiscus sabdariffa) *is boiled to make an exotic, deep garnet-colored beverage, served sweetened over ice. Large, graceful, and slightly acidic, fresh hibiscus petals can be added sparingly to salads, or they can be very lightly cooked. They also make gorgeous containers for diced fruit or vegetables. If fresh mangoes and papayas cannot be found, substitute other seasonal fruits. You can find banana or macadamia nut liqueur at fine liquor stores.*

Hawaiian Fruit Salad
with Hibiscus

Serves 4

1 mango
1 small papaya
1 small pineapple
Lime juice to taste
2 tablespoons candied ginger, finely diced
2 tablespoons banana or macadamia nut liqueur
2 hibiscus flowers, petals only, chopped
4 large hibiscus blossoms, stamens removed
Mint leaves, for garnish
Whole hibiscus, for garnish

Peel and finely dice the mango and papaya, discarding the seeds. Peel and finely dice the pineapple (you should have about 2 cups). Place the diced fruit in a large bowl. Add lime juice, diced ginger, and liqueur. Refrigerate the fruit to chill. Just before serving, toss in chopped petals. To serve, remove stamens from the whole hibiscus flowers. Set on dessert plates and spoon some of the fruit salad inside, letting the rest spill onto the plates, as you would a cornucopia. Decorate with mint leaves and additional petals. Serve immediately.

Lavender

*lthough it is usually sold under the name English lavender* (Lavandula officinalis), *there is no such thing according to* Rodale's Illustrated Encyclopedia of Herbs, *which lists the correct botanical name as L. angustifolia, a variety that also has medicinal applications as an expectorant and antispasmodic. At any rate, many experts still recommend "English" lavender for culinary purposes. In countries around the Mediterranean, where lavender originated, the dried flowers are used in the preparation of fragrant waters and vinegars, and sometimes custards. When picked at their prime and stripped from their stems, a pinch of diminutive blooms will add a mysterious scent to cookies, sorbets, and even beef stew!*

Lavender Shortbread

Makes 24 pieces

1 cup butter, at room temperature
½ cup granulated sugar
2 cups flour
Grated rind of ½ lemon
1 to 2 tablespoons fresh lavender blossoms, stripped from the stem
Additional blossoms, for garnish

In a large bowl, cream the butter and sugar until light and fluffy. Add the flour in increments, and blend until you obtain a smooth, firm dough. Mix in lemon rind and lavender blossoms. Line a flat surface with parchment paper. Divide the dough into two equal parts, and roll out into two 10 by 7-inch rectangles about ¼ inch thick. Place on a baking sheet and refrigerate dough a least 2 hours or overnight. When dough is cool, cut it into 1 by 3-inch rectangles. With a spatula, transfer them carefully onto a nonstick baking sheet, leaving an inch in between, because they expand as they cook. Discard parchment paper.

Preheat oven to 325°F. Bake for 18 to 20 minutes or until cookies turn light brown around the edges. Watch carefully so edges don't burn. (While dough is still warm, cut cookies into smaller pieces if desired.) Remove cookies from oven and let cool completely. To serve, sprinkle with additional lavender blossoms. To store, keep in an airtight container.

Lemon Verbena

n Europe and North Africa, the leaves and blossoms of the flowering shrub lemon verbena (Aloysia triphylla) *are usually steeped as an herb tea.* Lemon verbena traces its origins to Argentina and Chile, and like many other plants, owes its European debut to the discerning palate of early Spanish explorers. The bush can grow into a towering hedge, especially in mild climates. Don't be surprised if, after sipping a cup of lemon verbena tea, your eyelids begin to droop, because the plant is said to relax as well as to ease digestion. As its name implies, lemon verbena is characterized by its sweet, lemony scent.

My Favorite Herb Tea

Makes 1 cup

1 sprig fresh lemon verbena, blooms attached
1 cup boiling water
1 teaspoon sugar

In a small teapot or a mug, place a sprig of lemon verbena. Add 1 cup boiling water, and let tea brew for 2 to 3 minutes. Add sugar and enjoy.

Nasturtium

asturtium (Tropaeolum majus) *derives its name from the Latin words* nasus *and* toquere, *which translate as "nose twister"—no doubt in reference to its light, peppery smell. Some sources credit the Peruvians for introducing early Spanish explorers to the nasturtium and to its delightful taste. Others maintain that the edible qualities of the blossoms were already well known to the ancient Persians four centuries before Christ's birth. Whatever its origins, the nasturtium, perky and colorful in its varied shades of yellow and orange, ranks among the most popular edible flowers. The plants were first brought from Peru to Spain. From there, nasturtiums went on to seduce England, and then the rest of Europe. They require relatively little care in mild climates. When left whole, flowers can be stuffed with a sweet or a savory mousse. The peppery tang of the leaves brings to mind the taste of fresh watercress.*

Nasturtium Barley Shrimp Mold

Serves 6

4 cups chicken broth
1 cup raw barley
1 small cucumber, peeled, seeded, and finely diced
1 small sweet onion, very finely diced
½ red bell pepper, seeded and finely diced
6 to 8 small nasturtium leaves
6 nasturtium flowers
4 ounces precooked baby shrimp, rinsed and drained
1½ cups natural yogurt
2 teaspoons dry mustard
1 tablespoon lemon juice
1 tablespoon capers, drained
Salt and pepper to taste
Whole nasturtium flowers and leaves, for garnish

In a medium saucepan, bring chicken broth to a boil. Add barley, reduce heat to medium, cover, and cook until barley is tender, 40 to 45 minutes. Transfer to a large bowl and fluff with a fork.

Meanwhile, rinse, pat dry, and coarsely chop nasturtium leaves and petals. In a medium bowl, mix cucumber, onion, pepper, nasturtium leaves, nasturtium petals, and shrimp, and set aside. In a small bowl, mix yogurt, mustard, lemon juice, capers, and salt and pepper, and add to shrimp mixture. Blend in cooled barley, and adjust seasonings if necessary.

Lightly grease a 4-cup ring mold with vegetable oil. Press barley mixture into mold. Chill for 2 hours or overnight. To serve, unmold ring onto serving platter. Decorate with whole nasturtium flowers, encircling the base with whole nasturtium leaves. Serve chilled.

Passionflower

assionflower *(Passiflora species and cultivars), a native of Brazil, was named when missionaries and early Spanish explorers to Central America saw the stunning blossoms as* symbols of the Passion of Christ. The passionflower came to represent the crown of thorns. *Its ten petals symbolized the Apostles present at the Crucifixion, its three styles (threadlike female parts that are pollinated) the hammers used to drive the nails piercing Christ's hands and feet, and its five anthers the wounds He suffered. In season, the vines are laden with magnificent flowers in an exquisite array of colors. Passiflora* alata *yields a gorgeous blossom that makes a beautiful plate decoration.*

Passion fruit juice is sometimes available in specialty markets. To make fresh juice, slice ripe passion fruit in half and scoop the insides into a fine-meshed sieve set over a bowl. With a wooden spoon, press as much juice as possible through the sieve. Discard seeds and pulp. For this recipe, you may need up to a dozen fruit, depending upon the variety.

Passion Fruit Mousse

Makes Six ½-cup servings

1 envelope (¼ ounce) unflavored gelatin
½ cup plus 1 tablespoon sugar (or more to taste)
3 eggs, separated
1 cup passion fruit juice
½ pint heavy whipping cream
6 passionflowers, for garnish

In a medium saucepan set in a pan of simmering water, or in the top of a double boiler, mix gelatin with sugar. In a small bowl, whip egg yolks with passion fruit juice. Pour passion fruit liquid into sugar mixture and cook, stirring, until mixture thickens enough to coat the back of a wooden spoon. Remove from heat and transfer to a medium bowl. Refrigerate 40 to 50 minutes, or until gelatin attains the consistency of thick custard. Meanwhile, beat egg whites until stiff peaks form. In another bowl, beat whipping cream until soft peaks form. When gelatin has cooled, fold in beaten egg whites until thoroughly blended, then gently fold in whipped cream. At this point transfer mousse to a large serving bowl or 6 individual parfait glasses. Serve immediately or chill for 2 hours, until the mousse sets, and top with a fresh passionflower before serving.

Rose

symbol of beauty since time immemorial, the rose is thought to have originated in Persia, although differing theories abound. According to the ancient Greeks, the red rose, a symbol of passion, first bloomed when Aphrodite, the goddess of love, stuck her foot with a thorn and bled while assisting Adonis. For early Christians, the rose was a symbol of the Virgin Mary. They adorned cathedrals and church windows with the likeness of the flower. The first rosaries were strung with beads made from ground rose-petal paste. The fruit of the rose, or the rose hip, is a popular ingredient in herbal teas. Its vitamin-C content is so high that British sailors during World War II were encouraged to use it as a substitute for citrus.

Rose water
and rose syrup,
made from rose
petals, are used in
numerous Middle
Eastern and Indian
pastries and confections and
are available in some large super-
markets and in specialty stores.

Roses are generally propagated from
cuttings, although most home gardeners find they
achieve a higher rate of success by purchasing the
root stock or dormant plants suited to their particular
climate from a reputable nursery. Spring or fall is the
best time to plant roses. They demand greater care
than most other flowering bushes or shrubs, requiring
a sunny location and well-drained soil as well as the
judicious use of fertilizer and mulch. Rose petals are
best picked in summer, at the height of the blooming

Rose (cont.)

season before the flower opens completely. Grasp the flower by the stem, and pull off the petals all at once. Rinse them lightly under running water and set them on paper towels to drain. Handle them very gently so they don't bruise. Rose Damascena, Rosa gallica, *and* Rosa centifolia *are among the most fragrant.*

Rose Petal Sorbet

Serves 4

2 egg whites, at room temperature
1 teaspoon cream of tartar
1 cup water
1 cup loosely packed red rose petals, rinsed and patted dry
½ cup granulated sugar
4 teaspoons rose syrup
⅓ cup half-and-half
2 teaspoons lemon juice
Candied rose petals, for garnish (see page 58)

In a mixing bowl, beat the egg whites with the cream of tartar until stiff peaks form. Set aside.

In a small saucepan, combine the water and rose petals. Bring to a rolling boil. Remove from heat, and let steep, covered, for 10 minutes. With a slotted spoon, remove and discard rose petals. Add the sugar and rose syrup, and return to boil for 2 to 3 minutes. Immediately pour the boiling mixture in a slow stream into the egg whites, beating continuously. Add the half-and-half and lemon juice, and beat the mixture for 1 minute. Freeze until set, stirring several times during the freezing process to prevent the mixture from separating. To serve, spoon sorbet onto individual bowls, and garnish with candied rose petals.

Rosemary

he sweet flavor of rosemary (Rosmarinus officinalis), *whether fresh or dried, enhances the flavor of almost any Mediterranean dish.*
Indeed, many cooks in that part of the world add sprigs of rosemary to glowing coals to impart additional flavor to barbecued meats or fish. They also strip stems of their leaves and substitute them for conventional skewers.

A gift of rosemary connotes love, friendship, and remembrance. Students in ancient Greece wove garlands of rosemary in their hair, believing it would help improve their memory. During the Middle Ages, a sprig of rosemary placed under a pillow was thought to prevent bad dreams. The green, needlelike leaves of the perennial bush are among the world's most popular culinary herbs. Rosemary, a drought-tolerant plant, is also one of the easiest to grow, producing tiny blue blossoms that have a more delicate fragrance than the leaves. Use the blooms liberally to flavor stews, soups, and sorbets. A few fresh blossoms add an elegant touch to this simple pizza.

Rosemary Pizzette

Serves 2

2 five-inch premade pizza crusts
2 tablespoons virgin olive oil
2 medium tomatoes, thinly sliced
4 ounces shredded Fontina cheese
2 tablespoons rosemary blossoms

Preheat over to 350°F. With a small brush, paint crusts with olive oil. Line artfully with tomato slices. Sprinkle cheese and rosemary blossoms evenly over both crusts. Bake for 10 to 15 minutes or until cheese melts. Serve hot.

Safflower

n parts of the Middle East and in Mexico, dried safflower (Carthamus tinctorius) *is sometimes erroneously referred to as "real" Spanish saffron. In fact, safflower possesses neither the* pungent aroma nor the strong flavor that characterizes saffron (Crocus sativus), *the world's most expensive* spice. In this appetizer, safflower gives sweet fennel bulbs a faint golden tint and imparts a light, grassy aroma. Fennel, a staple of Mediterranean cuisine, is a lovely accompaniment to roasts or grilled meats, as well as a delicious topping for steamed couscous or rice. This dish is equally flavorful when served warm or at room temperature.

Braised Fennel with Safflower

Serves 4

2 tablespoons butter
2 large fennel bulbs
1 tablespoon fresh lemon juice
1 cup chicken broth
½ cup white wine
1 teaspoon crushed safflower
Salt and pepper to taste

In a heavy enamel saucepan or shallow frying pan, melt the butter over medium heat. Trim fennel bulbs of feathery fronds (reserve them to add flavor to a broth or a stew). Quarter the bulbs and place in saucepan, along with the lemon juice, chicken broth, white wine, and safflower. Cover tightly and simmer until bulbs are tender, 20 to 25 minutes. Remove lid and, using a slotted spoon, transfer the bulbs to a serving dish. Increase the heat to medium and continue to cook liquid until it is reduced by half. Pour over reserved bulbs. Season with salt and pepper. Serve warm or at room temperature.

Sage

age (Salvia rutilans), *also known as pineapple sage, is one of the "sacred" medicinal plants. Its name is derived from the Latin word* salvare, *meaning "safe" or "healthy." Many ancient* cultures believed sage possessed life-prolonging properties. Even today, the oil derived from sage has many recognized medicinal applications, including that of an antiseptic. Research has also shown that sage can reduce blood sugar in diabetics. In summer, the bright crimson flowers of the pineapple sage flutter like tiny butterflies on the end of each leafy limb. The leaves of culinary sage varieties have a light citrus taste that can be combined with stuffings, soups, or stews. Blossoms have a less pronounced flavor. The extremely strong taste of wild sage makes it unsuitable for cooking.*

Pineapple Sage Polenta Pies

Makes 8 to 10 pies

5 cups chicken broth
2 tablespoons finely diced sun-dried tomatoes
2 tablespoons butter
1½ cups polenta (yellow cornmeal)
½ cup grated Parmesan cheese (plus extra for garnish)
Freshly ground black pepper to taste
2 sage-flavored sausage links, crumbled
2 large onions, thinly sliced
2 tablespoons pineapple sage blossoms

In a large saucepan, combine chicken broth, sun-dried tomatoes, and butter, and bring to a boil. Add polenta in a stream, stirring continuously. Reduce heat to medium-low, stir in Parmesan cheese and pepper, partially cover to prevent splattering, and continue cooking until a wooden spoon stands upright in the center. Remove from heat.

Line an 11 by 13-inch baking sheet with foil, and lightly grease the foil with butter or vegetable oil. With a spatula, spread warm polenta mixture over baking sheet. Let it cool about 20 minutes. With a round 3- to 4-inch cookie-cutter, or with an inverted glass, press down on polenta to form rounds. With a spatula, transfer rounds to another baking sheet. Set aside.

Turn on oven to broil. Meanwhile, remove casings from sausages and cook with onions in a medium frying pan over medium-high heat. Cook until onions turn a light caramel color. Spoon equal amounts of sausage and onions atop each polenta pie. Sprinkle with Parmesan cheese. Broil for 2 or 3 minutes, watching carefully. Remove from oven. Sprinkle with sage flowers and serve immediately.

Society Garlic

ociety garlic (Tulbaghia violacea), with its mauve starlike blossoms, is commonly used as a border plant. Its strong aroma makes it a natural insect repellent. It is also a pungent addition, in moderate amounts, to butters, spreads, or any dish that calls for a touch of garlic. When brought indoors, the strong-scented cut flowers should be placed in a well-ventilated area because the odor can be overpowering! My friend Andrea Peterson, who farms organic lettuces and edible flowers in Fallbrook, California, assembles stunning salads when she tosses society garlic flowers with her specialty salad mix. This well-rounded dish could serve as the main course for an al fresco luncheon.

Andrea's Garden Salad
with Goat Cheese

Serves 4

4 cups baby greens, washed and dried
1 cup mixed flowers, such as calendula petals or viola, borage,
chive, or arugula blossoms, in any combination
½ cup olive oil
2 tablespoons rice vinegar or lemon juice
1 tablespoon water
2 teaspoons sugar
Salt and pepper to taste
½ cup chopped prunes
½ cup pine nuts
1 eight-ounce log goat cheese
½ cup plain bread crumbs
½ cup society garlic flowers, for garnish
1 French baguette, sliced

Preheat oven to 450°F. Place the baby greens and flowers in a salad bowl. Set aside. Make the dressing by whisking together in a small bowl the olive oil, vinegar or lemon juice, water, sugar, salt, and pepper. Toss the greens lightly with the dressing. Arrange salad in equal amounts on four salad plates. Top with prunes and pine nuts. Keep refrigerated. Meanwhile, slice the goat cheese into 4 equal parts. With a brush, lightly paint each side of cheese with a little olive oil and dredge on both sides with bread crumbs. Place the prepared slices on a nonstick baking sheet, and bake in the preheated oven for 5 minutes, until just softened. While still warm, place the cheese slices on the prepared greens and decorate with garlic flowers. Serve immediately with slices of crisp baguette bread.

Sunflower

A colorful member of the daisy family, sunflowers (Helianthus annuus), can grow to be twelve feet tall! The sunflower can be traced back to Latin America, where the Incas of Peru revered it as an earthly representation of their sun god. These days, sunflowers are an important financial crop in such European countries as Belgium and France, principally for the oil extracted from the seeds. Sunflower buds, according to ancient herbal books, were once considered aphrodisiacs. If left unopened, sunflower buds can be steamed, or boiled like artichokes until they are tender, and tossed with butter or a tangy vinaigrette dressing.

Raw sunflower petals have a slightly bitter taste, and for this reason I prefer to steam them lightly.

Sunflower Pasta Salad

Serves 4 to 6

2 chicken breasts, skin removed
½ cup bottled teriyaki marinade
8 ounces fresh pasta
1 eight-ounce bottle Italian dressing
¼ cup toasted sunflower seeds
Petals from 2 sunflowers
6 shredded basil leaves, if desired

In a medium bowl, combine the chicken with the marinade. Let it stand, turning once or twice, for 20 to 30 minutes. Turn the oven to broil. Drain the chicken breasts. Place them in a baking dish or on a baking sheet, and broil 3 to 4 minutes on each side, until the chicken is cooked through. Remove from the oven and let cool. Cut the chicken into ½-inch strips and set aside.

In a large pan filled with lightly salted boiling water, cook pasta until al dente, 2 to 3 minutes. Drain well. Rinse under cold water and drain again. Transfer to a serving bowl and toss with dressing and sunflower seeds. Set aside. In a steamer set atop boiling water, steam petals for 2 minutes. Remove from heat. To assemble salad, mound pasta on serving platter. Top artfully with steamed petals and strips of chicken. Chill for 1 hour. Sprinkle with basil before serving.

Tulip

 istorians differ as to the origins of the tulip (Tulipa *species and cultivars*) tracing them back to Turkey or Persia. These days, however, tulips are most often associated with the Netherlands. The Dutch passion for tulips reached its apogee in the seventeenth century when speculators trading in the precious bulbs amassed great fortunes. As the bulbs made their way onto the marketplace, their overinflated value decreased, and the tulip eventually became a ubiquitous fixture of the Dutch national landscape. Tulips were once more a precious commodity during World War II, when much of the Dutch population survived by eating boiled tulip bulbs. Still today, much of the Netherlands' economy relies on the growing and exporting of the bulbs. Tulips prefer cooler climes, bursting into bloom at the first touch of spring. However, many varieties are acclimatized to grow in warmer areas.

The dramatic blossoms make beautiful edible cups for fruit sorbets, sweet or savory mousses, or finely minced, crisp vegetables. Their delicately fresh sweetness is especially prevalent in the white, peach, or pink blooms, which are ideally suited for this chocolate mousse filling.

Chocolate-Moussed Tulips

Serves 8

4 ounces semisweet chocolate
⅓ cup sweet butter
2 egg yolks
2 tablespoons Grand Marnier
3 egg whites, at room temperature (see note below)
½ teaspoon cream of tartar
2 teaspoons sugar
Grated zest of half an orange
8 tulips, rinsed and dried
3 pints raspberries, rinsed and drained

In the top of a double boiler, melt the chocolate until smooth. Stir in the butter, remove from heat, and allow to cool a few minutes. Stir in the egg yolks, one at a time, and the Grand Marnier. Set aside.

In a medium bowl, beat the egg whites with cream of tartar until fairly stiff. Halfway through, add the sugar and continue beating until stiff peaks form. With a spatula, carefully fold the chocolate mixture into the beaten egg whites. Stir in orange zest. Refrigerate 10 to 15 minutes.

Meanwhile, prepare tulips for filling. Carefully push petals apart, and with a small pair of scissors, cut out pistil and stamen. Cut off the stem. Take mousse from refrigerator and fill each blossom three-quarters full, gently holding the petals. Mound 1 or 2 tablespoons of mousse in the bottom of each of 6 or 8 dessert cups. Press a filled tulip into each mound so that it remains upright in the cup. Surround tulips with an even amount of raspberries. Set a raspberry in the center of each tulip. Chill until ready to serve.

Note: When using eggs, make sure they come from a reliable source, store them in the refrigerator, and use them before the expiration date printed on the carton. Pregnant women and immunodeficient patients should refrain from eating raw egg whites.

Viola

 he aptly named multicolored violas (Viola tricolor), *or Johnny-jump-ups,* pop up year after year in endless succession. Violas and violets are part of the same Violaceae *family, as are* pansies. They have a faint yet distinctive sweet taste. In A Midsummer Night's Dream, *Shakespeare assigns aphrodisiacal properties to the lovely bloom, which legend has it, was favored by Cupid, the god of love. Once called Heartease, violas figured prominently in apothecaries' love potions. Stephenie Caughlin, the owner of Seabreeze Organic Farm, and Jan Sayles of Edible Acres, both in Southern California, have found a more up-to-date use for violas, tossing them in their spring lettuce mix.*
Another way Stephenie enjoys these kaleidoscopic blossoms is to encase them in ice to make "blooming" ice cubes. She freezes them in ice cube trays or a ring mold and adds them as decoration to her punch bowl.

Stephenie's Blooming Ice Cubes

25–30 freshly picked violas
Ice cube trays or ice ring

The day before use, fill ice cube trays (or ring mold) halfway up with water. Freeze 3 to 4 hours. Layer flowers over ice and cover with more water. Freeze until set.

Violet

ike faithful friends, tiny violet blossoms (Viola odorata *or English violet*) *reappear every year, dotting shady patches of ground with their delicate purple touch. Herbalists and gourmet gardeners both treasure this springtime flower, which, legend has it, originally sprung from the tears of the goddess Isis.*

Although violets have been cultivated since ancient times, it seems the lavender-colored blossoms reached the peak of their popularity during the Victorian era, when they brightened bridal nosegays and lent their unmistakable scent to syrups and jellies. Violets were also known for their medicinal and antiseptic properties, and were commonly used in antiseptics. My friend Luna Rose, an herbal consultant, serves this wonderful concoction over ice cream, and also uses it to help soothe a sore throat. Add a little violet syrup to a glass of lemonade for an exotic and romantic drink. Toss white blossoms in a salad, or use them to decorate a special dessert.

Luna's Violet Syrup

Makes 1¹/₄ cups

1 cup violet blossoms, stems removed
1¼ cups distilled water
2 tablespoons lemon juice
2 cups granulated sugar

Rinse and gently pat dry violet blossoms. In a small saucepan, bring distilled water to a boil. Place blossoms in a heatproof, sterilized pint jar, and cover with boiling water. Let steep 24 hours. The next day, strain through cheesecloth or fine-meshed sieve, and discard blossoms. Stir in lemon juice. Place infusion in a saucepan and bring to a boil. Add sugar, stirring continually. Bring to a rolling boil and continue to boil until the liquid registers 230°F on a candy thermometer. With a metal spoon, skim off foam. Remove from heat and, using a funnel, pour into a sterilized bottle or jar. Cap tightly. Use as a topping for ice cream. The syrup will keep for 2 to 3 months in the refrigerator.

Yucca

he yucca (Yucca elephantipes), *an exotic member of the agave family, is a native of the American South-west and is also known as Spanish bayonet. Native Americans and Latin Americans have long put yucca varieties to a multitude of uses, from stem to bloom. They separated the fibrous leaves into fine strands to use for sewing. They boiled the asparagus-like heart of the stem, and also savored the crunchy, fresh-tasting blossoms, raw or cooked. The distinctive, cream-colored bells of the towering yucca plant burst into bloom in temperate zones in early fall. When eaten raw, the petals (separated from the bitter center parts) add a light, exotic crunch to cooked vegetable dishes or salads. They can also be parboiled or used in stir-fries.*

Stir-Fried Yucca with Sugar Snap Peas

Serves 2

½ pound sweet sugar snap or snow peas
2 tablespoons butter
Petals from 6 to 8 yucca blossoms, cut into thin strips
Pinch of sugar
Salt to taste

Remove strings from snap peas and rinse pods. In a medium
frying pan, melt butter over medium-high heat. Add snap peas
and stir-fry 2 to 3 minutes. Add yucca petals, sugar, and salt, and
stir-fry 1 to 2 minutes. Serve immediately.

Zucchini

he blossoms of zucchini (Cucurbita pepo *species and cultivars), with their mild zucchini flavor, are served as a side dish in Mexico and around the Mediterranean. In Italy and France, the individual flowers are often stuffed or dipped in batter and deep-fried. Blossoms are also chopped, lightly sautéed, and served wrapped inside warm tortillas in Mexico. Zucchini plants bear both male and female flowers. Female flowers are recognizable by the slight swelling at their base, which will eventually develop into a vegetable. Left whole, zucchini blossoms are a lovely addition to frittatas or quiches.*

Zucchini Blossom Frittata

Serves 4

24 fresh zucchini blossoms, rinsed and gently shaken dry
⅓ cup flour
½ teaspoon salt
¼ teaspoon pepper
3 tablespoons olive oil
6 eggs
4 sun-dried tomato halves, finely chopped
1 teaspoon fresh thyme leaves (or ½ teaspoon dried)
2 tablespoons grated Parmesan cheese
Wedges of lemon

Reserve 6 blossoms for garnish. In a paper or plastic bag, place the remaining zucchini blossoms, flour, salt, and pepper. Shake until blossoms are evenly coated.

In a 9-inch (preferably nonstick) frying pan, heat olive oil over medium-high heat. Sauté blossoms until golden, stirring occasionally, 5 to 6 minutes. Meanwhile, in a large bowl, beat the eggs, and stir in the chopped tomatoes, thyme, and Parmesan cheese. Pour egg mixture over sautéed zucchini blossoms. Reduce heat to medium, and cook, partially covered, for 2 to 3 minutes. With a spatula, lift sides of frittata to let uncooked egg slide down the sides and continue cooking until top of frittata is set. Then, carefully flip frittata over onto a dinner plate. Gently slide frittata back into pan, and cook other side until lightly golden. To serve, slide the frittata, blossom-side up, onto a serving platter, and decorate with remaining fresh blossoms. Serve with wedges of lemon.

Additional Recipes

Crystallized Flower Petals

Makes enough for 20 large petals

Violets, borage, dianthus, or rose petals can all be candied using this recipe. Miniature roses can also be candied whole and used as the crowning touch for elegant cakes. Pick flowers when they are at the peak of their blooming cycle, and handle them very gently. Make enough for a year-round supply to decorate cakes and puddings or to give as a special edible gift!

I use this method to candy flowers because it uses no raw egg whites. The petals keep their shape very well. Gum Arabic is a fine powder derived from an acacia tree native to the Sudan and Egypt. You can find it in baking and candy supply stores. When candying rose petals, use rose water instead of water for additional flavor. For citrus petals, substitute orange blossom water (for more information, see page 14).

1 tablespoon gum Arabic
1 tablespoon warm water
20 rose petals, gently rinsed and patted dry
1/4 cup superfine sugar

In a small bowl, with a wooden spoon, thoroughly mix the gum Arabic with the water until smooth. If small lumps remain, strain the mixture through a fine-meshed sieve. With a clean, small, soft-bristle brush, paint both sides of a petal with a thin coat of the gum Arabic mixture. Sprinkle each side lightly with superfine sugar. Set petal on a metal rack to air dry. Continue in this manner until all the ingredients are used. When the petals are completely dry, store them in an airtight container. Use within 3 months.

Jeanne's Lavender Lemonade

Jeanne Dunn and her husband, Chris, often prepare gallons of this refreshing lemonade for the customers who flock to their biannual herb festival at their Herban Garden nursery in Rainbow, California. The friendly couple, who have been in the herb business since 1983, grow herbs and edible flowers for commercial distribution. Large bushes of lavender dot their nursery. Jeanne is especially fond of sweet lavender and the "English" lavender varieties, which she finds best suited for this refreshing drink.

5 cups water
½ cup lavender flowers, stripped from stems
⅓ cup freshly squeezed lemon juice
½ cup granulated sugar, or more to taste
Mint leaves, for garnish

In a small saucepan on the stove, bring 1 cup water to a rolling boil. Remove from heat and add lavender flowers. Cover and steep for 10 minutes. Strain through a fine-meshed sieve, discard blossoms, and set lavender tea aside. Meanwhile, in a quart jug, mix lemon juice with 4 cups water and sugar to taste. Add prepared lavender tea. Refrigerate until chilled. Serve in tall glasses over ice cubes and decorate with mint leaves.

Rose Syrup Lemonade
with Rose-Scented Ice Cubes

Makes 1 quart

This lemonade is even prettier and more fragrant when served with rose-scented ice cubes. To make the ice cubes, double the lemonade recipe, and freeze half of it in ice cube trays.

⅓ cup freshly squeezed lemon juice
4 cups cold water
½ cup granulated sugar, or to taste
3 teaspoons rose syrup, or to taste (see page 35)
Small rose on a stem, cleaned, for garnish

In a quart jug, mix lemon juice with water, sugar, and rose syrup. Stir well. To serve, pour lemonade over rose-scented ice cubes and garnish with a small, fresh rose on a stem. Serve with a straw.

Violet Lemonade

Makes 1 quart

¼ cup lemon juice
4 cups water
¼ cup sugar
⅓ cup Luna's Violet Syrup (page 53)
Stephanie's Blooming Ice Cubes, for garnish (page 51)
Fresh violets, for garnish

In a large jug, mix lemon juice, water, and sugar. Stir in prepared syrup. Serve in tall glasses over ice cubes. Garnish with fresh violets. Serve with a straw.

More Edible Flowers

*Only flowers grown without pesticides may be
eaten, and they should be enjoyed in moderation.
When in doubt, consult a horticultural specialist or an
encyclopedia of edible plants (see Bibliography).*

Artichoke *(Cynara scolymus):* This plump
globe is the crown of the cynara plant. Dip
meaty flesh at base of leaves in melted butter or
creamy dressing.

Banana *(Musa paradisiaca):* The
whole purple blossom and the bracts,
which hold the flowers, are edible.
Slice, parboil, and drain before adding
to curries or stir-fries.

Carnation *(Dianthus caryophyllus*
species and cultivars): Steep in wine,
candy, or use as cake decoration. Remove
petals from calyx and snip off bitter
white base before using.

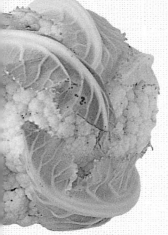

Cauliflower *(Brassica oleracea* var. *botrytis):* This member of the cabbage family is a flower in its own right. Whether consumed raw or cooked, it is one of our most common "vegetables."

Chinese chives *(Allium tuberosum):* The delicate, white, star-shaped flowers have a slight garlic fragrance. Flowers as well as stems are edible, raw or cooked.

Chrysanthemum (*Chrysanthemum* species and cultivars): Flowers vary in color from bright yellow to deep rust, and in flavor from mild to bitter. Taste before using. Briefly blanch petals before adding to Chinese-style stir-fries or tossing in small amounts with salad greens.

Cornflower *(Centaurea cyanus):* Also called bachelor's button, this azure bloom is a natural food dye and is commonly used as a garnish. In Germany, cornflower is used to make a popular liqueur.

Dandelion *(Taraxacum officinale):* This common weed, a hardy perennial and member of the daisy family, has long been savored as a tasty green, either raw or cooked. Its name derives from the French *dent de lion,* meaning "lion's tooth," because of the jagged shape of the leaves. Dandelion blossoms are often turned into wine, and dried, ground roots can be used as a coffee substitute.

Feijoa or pineapple guava *(Feijoa sellowiana):* A relative of the true guava, *feijoa's* popular name is pineapple guava. *Feijoa* blossoms appear in early summer and are not only lovely to look at, with their pale pink petals set off by a frilly crown of red anthers, but they are also one of the most flavorful flowers, tasting much like the ripe fruit that develops a few weeks later.

Fuchsia *(Fuchsia* species and cultivars): Blooms have no distinct flavor. Their explosive colors and graceful shape are ideal for garnishing a finished dish.

Gardenia *(Gardenia jasmi-noides):* The intensely fragrant, light cream-colored blossom is used for decorative purposes. In the Far East, dried gardenia blossoms are used to impart their heady scent to jasmine tea.

Honeysuckle *(Lonicera japonica):* This climbing vine has lovely white or pale yellow flowers filled with a syrupy-sweet nectar. Flowers can be candied whole or used as cake decorations.

Ornamental kale *(Brassica oleracea):* Stunning, frilly leaves have intense purple colors tinged with green. Favored by upscale chefs as a backdrop for foods.

Lily (*Lilium* species and cultivars): Chop or slice petals, and sprinkle sparingly on salads, omelets, or soups. The petals don't have an assertive flavor, but do have a crunchy texture.

Sweet marigold *(Tagetes lucida):* This is sometimes called Spanish, Mexican, or winter tarragon. The flavor of the leaves and the dainty yellow blossoms is similar to that of French tarragon. Add them sparingly to herb vinegars, or use them in dressings and dishes calling for French tarragon.

Mint (*Mentha* species and cultivars): Over 600 varieties of mint have been catalogued, but not all of them are edible. Spearmint and peppermint, the two most popular varieties, add their distinctive fragrance to a cornucopia of products and also, to foods the world over. Mint tea, brewed from fresh spearmint leaves and dried Chinese green tea leaves, is popular throughout North Africa.

Iceland poppy *(Papaver nudicaule):*
Brilliant red- or orange-hued petals
have slightly bitter taste. Use sparingly
as garnish. Do not confuse with opium
poppy *(Papaver somniferum),* which is
illegal to grow in the United States.

Thyme *(Thymus* species and cultivars):
This lovely herb comes in endless
varieties, including lemon and pineapple. Diminutive blue flowers add a
light, distinctive scent to soups and
stews.

Sources and Experts

Araiza-Smith Specialty Growers, Rancho Las Lomas, San Miguel de las Minas, Baja California, Mexico. (619) 794-0570. *Organically grown herbs and flowers for culinary and medicinal uses.*

Cordon Bleu Farms, P.O. Box 2033, San Marcos, CA 92079. *Specializes in daylilies. Queries by mail only.*

Edible Acres, 2252 Catalina Avenue, Vista, CA 92084. (619) 758-1030. *Specializes in violas, nasturtiums, and fuschia blossoms.*

Exotica Rare Fruit Nursery, 2508-B East Vista Way, Vista, CA 92084. (619) 724-9093. *Rare trees and fruits, including passion fruit.*

The Greenhouse, P.O. Box 231069, Encinitas, CA 92023-1069. (619) 942-5371. *One of the largest suppliers of herbs and edible flowers in the United States. Distributes to supermarkets nationwide.*

The Herban Garden, 5002 Second Street, Rainbow, CA 92028. (619) 723-2967. *Specializes in herbs and ornamentals. Mail order.*

Maxi Flowers à la Carte, 1015 Martin Lane, Sebastopol, CA 95472. (707) 829-0592. *Specializes in organically grown edible flowers. Mail order.*

Multiflora, 522 Beaumont Drive, Vista, CA 92084. (619) 758-3913. *Specializes in herbs and edible flowers.*

Nature's Nursery: A Natural Farm, 2421 Majella Road, Vista, CA 92084. (619) 630-1404. *Ornamentals and edible flowers.*

New Leaf Nurseries, 2456 Foothill Drive, Vista, CA 92084. (619) 726-9269. *Specializes in all types of geraniums. Mail order.*

Ornamental Edibles, Specialty Seeds by Mail, 3622 Weedin Court, San Jose, CA 95132. (408) 946-SEED. *Edible flower seeds. Mail order.*

Peterson and Pio Specialty Produce, 5910 Camino Baja Cerro, Fallbrook, CA 92028. (619) 439-6466. *Organically grown herbs and edible flowers.*

Rose, Luna, 1666 Independence Way, Vista, CA 92084. (619) 724-6590. *Teacher and herbalist.*

Seabreeze Organic Farm, 3909 Arroyo Sorrento Road, San Diego, CA 92130. (619) 481-2890. *Specializes in exotic greens and edible flowers.*

Seeds of Change, Organic Seeds, 621 Old Santa Fe Trail, #10, Santa Fe, NM 87501. (505) 983-8956. *Catalog lists dozens of open-pollinated edible flowers.*

Shepherd's Garden Seeds, Felton, CA 95018. (408) 335-6910. *Catalog lists dozens of varieties of edible flowers.*

Voss, Gilbert, 1950 Parkside Drive, Eugene, OR 97403. (503) 334-6191. *Botanical consultant.*

Weidners' Gardens, 695 Normandy Street, Encinitas, CA 92024. (619) 436-2194. *Specializes in begonias. Mail order.*

Bibliography

Cowhurst, Adrienne. *The Flower Cookbook.* New York: Lancer Books, 1973.

De Belder-Kovacic, Jelena and Elisabeth de Lestrieux. *La Saveur des Fleurs: A la découverte de la Cuisine aux Fleurs.* (Duculot, Paris, éditeur, 1991)

Facciola, Stephen. *Cornucopia: A Sourcebook of Edible Plants.* Vista, CA: Kampong Publications, 1990. (Write Kampong Publications, 1870 Sunrise Drive, Vista, CA 92084 to obtain.)

Hendrickson, Robert. *Lewd Food: The Complete Guide to Aphrodisiac Edibles.* Radnor, PA: Chilton Book Co., 1974.

Hutson, Lucinda. *The Herb Garden Cookbook.* Houston: Gulf Publishing, 1992.

Meyer, Joseph E. *The Herbalist.* Hammond, IN: Hammond Book Co., 1934.

Ody, Penelope. *The Complete Medicinal Herbal.* New York: Dorling Kindersley, 1993.

Ortiz, Elizabeth Lambert. *The Encyclopedia of Herbs, Spices & Flavorings.* New York: Dorling Kindersley, 1992.

Rodale Press staff and William H. Hylton. *Rodale's Illustrated Encyclopedia of Herbs.* Emmaus, PA: Rodale Press, 1987.

Rogers, Ford B. *Citrus: A Cookbook.* New York: Simon and Schuster, 1993.

Shaudys, Phyllis V. *Herbal Treasures: Inspiring Month-by-Month Projects for Gardening, Cooking & Crafts.* Pownal, VT: Garden Way Publishing, 1990.

Smith, Leona Woodring. *The Forgotten Art of Flower Cookery.* Gretna, LA: Pelican Publishing, 1973.

Sweet, Muriel. *Common Edible & Useful Plants of the West.* Rev. ed. Happy Camp, CA: Naturegraph Publishers, Inc., 1976.

Index